Dyspraxia

A Parent's Guide to Understanding Dyspraxia in Children and How to Help a Dyspraxic Child

by Cassandra Simmons

Table of Contents

Introduction 1

Chapter 1: Understanding Dyspraxia 7

Chapter 2: Identifying the Tell-Tale Signs 15

Chapter 3: How Dyspraxia Is Diagnosed 25

Chapter 4: How a Parent Can Help from Home ... 31

Chapter 5: A Parent's Journey ~ Coping Advice for Parents 39

Conclusion 45

Introduction

Is your child unusually clumsy? Does he have difficulty holding his spoon or fork properly when eating? Does his room look like a tornado just swept through? Is he having trouble with the basics of movement and coordination? Dyspraxia is a medical condition that affects many, often times without the parents even being aware of what the condition is. It is a disorder that is all too real and can greatly affect the life of the afflicted as well as the lives of their loved ones.

Nevertheless, if your child is diagnosed early enough and gets some extra help from you along the way, there is a good chance that he can manage the dyspraxia and live a perfectly normal and happy life. As a parent, you're going to need all the information you can get to better understand your child's condition so that you can learn how to help. Furthermore, having a full understanding of dyspraxia will also make it easier for siblings and other family members to adjust and accommodate your child's needs.

This book is going to provide you with lots of important information about dyspraxia, its causes, symptoms, and effects. And most importantly, you'll gain plenty of information on how you can help support your child in the process of managing his dyspraxia while living a quality life.

© Copyright 2015 by Miafn LLC - All rights reserved.

This document is geared towards providing reliable information in regards to the topic and issue covered. The publication is sold with the idea that the publisher is not required to render accounting, officially permitted, or otherwise, qualified services. If advice is necessary, legal or professional, a practiced individual in the profession should be ordered.

- From a Declaration of Principles which was accepted and approved equally by a Committee of the American Bar Association and a Committee of Publishers and Associations.

In no way is it legal to reproduce, duplicate, or transmit any part of this document in either electronic means or in printed format. Recording of this publication is strictly prohibited and any storage of this document is not allowed unless with written permission from the publisher. All rights reserved.

The information provided herein is stated to be truthful and consistent, in that any liability, in terms of inattention or otherwise, by any usage or abuse of any policies, processes, or directions contained within is solely and completely the responsibility of the recipient reader. Under no circumstances will any legal responsibility or blame be held against the publisher for any reparation, damages, or monetary loss due to the information herein, either directly or indirectly.

Respective authors own all copyrights not held by the publisher.

The information herein is offered for informational purposes solely, and is universal as so. The presentation of the information is without contract or any type of guarantee assurance.

The trademarks that are used are without any consent, and the publication of the trademark is without permission or backing by the trademark owner. All trademarks and brands within this book are for clarifying purposes only and are the owned by the owners themselves, not affiliated with this document.

Chapter 1: Understanding Dyspraxia

Many people are unfamiliar with dyspraxia. However, many of us have seen individuals who seem to always have trouble planning and coordinating their physical movement. Have you ever wondered why some people are extraordinarily clumsy? And what conclusions have we made about people who have speech problems? For those who have not heard of dyspraxia, it's easy to label these individuals as "clownish", "graceless", or "boorish". People even conclude that these persons have low intelligence. However, what we need to understand is that dyspraxia has nothing to do with low intelligence and muscle weakness. There is more to know and understand about this ailment.

The Medical Condition Called Dyspraxia

To put it simply, dyspraxia is a motor planning disorder. In layman's terms, it is sometimes described as the 'clumsy-child syndrome' although there is definitely more to it than that. Those in the medical profession find it more accurate to call it a developmental coordination difficulty or DCD. It is described as having the inability to plan and coordinate physical movements. This is a neurological disorder wherein the messages sent by the brain are not accurately received by the body.

Children who suffer from this disorder may have problems with balance, posture, and speech. Unfortunately, many parents fail to detect these signs early because young children are naturally clumsy and are not always very verbal as they are still developing their speech ability. Parents will generally notice the symptoms of dyspraxia more clearly as the child grows older. For example, children may be unable to move and coordinate their tongue and mouth in order to create the correct phonetic sounds when talking. Thus, their speech is slurred and they have difficulty expressing themselves. A 10-year old child with dyspraxia may have trouble walking and jumping. At school he may have difficulty holding a pen and writing.

Due to these symptoms, a child with dyspraxia may have trouble making friends and socializing. His stunted social skills results in immature conduct that make those around him conclude that he has low intelligence. In reality, most individuals with dyspraxia possess average to above-average IQ. Dyspraxia is also a permanent condition. Parents should never think that their child will outgrow it. The good news is that the symptoms of dyspraxia can be managed through physical, speech and occupational therapy.

With professional assistance, coupled with patience and understanding from loving parents, a child with dyspraxia will be able to work around the limitations caused by the condition and put more focus on developing his strengths.

Unfortunately, dyspraxia may go hand in hand with other disorders such as Asperger's syndrome, ADHD, and dyslexia. These conditions are known to affect a child's development and can lead to learning difficulties. An early diagnosis can do wonders to a child's social and communication development. Parents and teachers can also adjust to the child's condition by making the home and school more accommodating to the child with dyspraxia.

If you think that your kid may be suffering from this neurological disorder, have him checked by a medical professional as soon as possible. Remember that the earlier he is diagnosed and helped, the bigger his chances of leading a healthier and happier life. As parents, it is your duty to get him all the help he needs.

The Types of Dyspraxia

Children with dyspraxia will exhibit different symptoms. One child's symptoms are never exactly the same as another. This is because different kinds of movement are affected by the disorder. Here are the most common kinds of dyspraxia:

Constructional Dyspraxia

In this type of dyspraxia, the child is unable to use the hands to create or build anything using building blocks. If asked to copy or draw a geometric figure, he may be unable to do so even if he knows how to do it and wants to do it.

Ideational Dyspraxia

In this kind of dyspraxia, the child is unable to complete tasks that require them to follow a sequence. They may not be able to brush their teeth, take a bath, or set the table.

Oromotor Dyspraxia

A child diagnosed with Oromotor Dyspraxia cannot pronounce words correctly because he is unable to coordinate muscle movement in the mouth.

Ideomotor Dyspraxia

This type is characterized by the inability of the child to do a task upon request or to translate ideas into motion. For instance, he may be able to comb his hair every morning, but if you tell him to do this task at a random moment, he may not be able to do it. He knows how to wave his hand but will have trouble doing it when told to do so.

The Occurrence of Dyspraxia

Dyspraxia is fairly common although it is not as widespread as dyslexia. It affects six to ten percent of children, occurring more in boys than in girls. Dyspraxia is not a new medical condition; it has been affecting many individuals for a long time. Nevertheless, most people who suffer from it are not properly diagnosed and go on to live their lives never knowing that they are afflicted with it.

Until today, the exact cause of this neurological disorder is unknown although experts are considering heredity, the effects of alcohol intake by pregnant women, premature birth, and low birth weights.

Chapter 2: Identifying the Tell-Tale Signs

Dyspraxia can be detected easily when the parent is knowledgeable of its symptoms. However, many parents miss the signs because young children are normally clumsy and their speech is not yet fully developed. Nevertheless, there are warning signs that indicate a neurological disorder. Here's what parents need to know about the symptoms of dyspraxia.

The Symptoms

Among the reasons why dyspraxia is detected late or is not detected at all are its varying symptoms. When it comes to this medical condition, there is no typical dyspraxia patient. Every child exhibits symptoms that are unique from those of others. In some children, the symptoms are mild while in others, severe.

Indications in Children—Up to 1 year

- Irritable
- Do not feed well
- Unable to sit up at 6 months

- Late to crawl, stand up or walk

Indications in Children—Age 2 to 3 years

- Delayed speech
- Potty training problems
- Inability to ride a bike
- Don't like to play with blocks and puzzles
- Can't throw or catch a ball
- Difficulty in holding fork and spoon
- Prefer to eat using fingers
- Messy eaters

Indications in Children—Age 3 to 6 years

- Do not jump
- Unable to hop or skip around
- Can talk but words are not clear
- Talk slowly and softly
- Have problems playing with other kids

- Have trouble with zippers, buttons, and snaps
- Unable to grasp objects
- Lose balance
- Can't catch a ball
- Prone to bumping into things
- Fail to show right or left hand dominance
- Can't hold crayons or pencils
- Unable to write legibly
- Unable to sit up straight on a chair

Indications in Children—Age 7 to 13 years

- Difficulty in writing
- Difficulty in gripping objects such as spoons, forks, and pens
- Unable to form letters when writing
- Have weak muscle tone
- Struggle with physical activities
- Have problems with tasks that require hand-eye coordination

- Unable to remember instructions and so aren't able to follow them

- Difficulty in moving objects from point A to B

- May not be able to stay focused on tasks at hand

Indications in Children—Age 14 to 18 years

- Prone to losing personal stuff

- Forgetfulness

- Sloppy speech

- Struggle with sports and gym class

- Prone to falling, bumping, tripping

- Difficulty jumping

- Unable to ride a bike

- Can't comprehend nonverbal communication

- Have difficulty completing tasks that require sequencing

- Can't work on tasks that are timed

- Illegible handwriting

- Difficulty concentrating

Parents who observe these symptoms in their child will certainly be pained, knowing that their child has limited abilities compared to other kids his age. However, every parent should know that most of these symptoms can be managed. With professional treatment and support, the child with dyspraxia can lead a normal life. I can never overemphasize the big difference it makes for kids with dyspraxia to be lovingly given the help they need.

Another thing that parents need to know is the fact that children afflicted with dyspraxia are usually of average or above-average intelligence. Because of their mental awareness, the limitations brought on by the condition can cause a great deal of frustration for the child. For example, a child with dyspraxia will be able to verbalize his excellent ideas but will have trouble writing all of them down. If children with dyspraxia are not given treatment and professional help, they will become frustrated and tend to give up trying to do the things they want to accomplish. They might even stop brushing their teeth, taking a shower, or making their bed if they find it too difficult to do. Parents of these kids need to help them early, so that they will be able to function in society as competent adults.

Skills Affected by Dyspraxia

Because the messages and commands from the brain are not transmitted accurately to the body, a number of skills are affected when a person has dyspraxia. It's crucial to keep in mind that all of these areas can be improved with professional help, plus the love and understanding of parents and siblings.

Academics

When a child with dyspraxia remains undiagnosed and is not given professional help for the condition, the child will experience a difficult time in school. He will have trouble with holding a pen, writing, reading, spelling, and talking. If the teacher has no knowledge about this medical condition, it would be easy for her to assume that the child has a low IQ. He could also be subject to ridicule and bullying by classmates.

Communication Skills

The child with dyspraxia will be unable to control his tongue and mouth muscles. As a result, he is unable to enunciate words. His speech is slurred and it can be hard to understand what he is saying. He will find it very frustrating that those around him don't understand him. Parents, siblings, and teachers who are trained to handle kids with dyspraxia will be able to help the child with dyspraxia to express himself verbally. However, if the people around the child don't know about the condition, they may get just as frustrated and as a result, they might ignore the child, refrain from speaking to him, or just walk away when they can't understand what he's saying.

It goes without saying that a child in this situation will be greatly affected. He may either clam up or only talk when it is absolutely necessary. The parents at this point must arrange to have the child undergo speech therapy. It also becomes imperative for those around the child to be educated about dyspraxia so that they can exercise more patience when interacting with him or her. Unfortunately, it is not only the clarity of words that is affected in dyspraxia. The child will likely also have trouble adjusting the volume and pitch of his voice.

Social Skills

Children with dyspraxia manifest various symptoms that limit their movement. They are pretty much unable to engage in physical activities while at play and in school. Some will find it difficult to jump, skip, ride a bicycle, catch and throw a ball, etc. A child with dyspraxia who is not able to do these activities with other kids his age will typically fall behind socially. Young kids socialize when they are playing. They do activities together and they communicate. Unfortunately, the child's physical limitations and speech difficulties will affect his ability to socialize and make friends.

Behavioral Skills

Acting out on his frustration and his lack of social skills, the child with dyspraxia may seem immature. Again, parents and other family members need to be more understanding and must always exercise a great deal of patience when relating to the child with dyspraxia.

Emotional Skills

Without effective speech therapy, the child with dyspraxia may not be able to express his feelings and emotions verbally. It is physically difficult for him to talk to someone about how he feels and as a result, his emotions can get bottled-up. Parents should encourage the child to always express how they feel even when talking might be difficult for them. The lack of social interaction with people can also affect the emotional skills of the child with dyspraxia.

Overall Life Skills

At an early age, young children are taught tasks that can help them become independent. However, a child with dyspraxia will have difficulty mastering these tasks. These include routine everyday tasks like brushing his teeth, making the bed, taking a bath, dressing up, etc. It is with the patience and support of loving parents that a child with dyspraxia will be able to do these everyday tasks on his own. It might take a long time, but he will become independent, especially if he receives continuous and regular physical therapy as well as the other treatments that he needs in order to function with self-sufficiency.

Chapter 3: How Dyspraxia Is Diagnosed

All parents observe their children during the developmental stages and they are mostly aware of what their child can and can't do. However, there are parents who are overly concerned with their kid's capabilities even when all seems normal. On the other hand, there are also parents who veer towards denial when they see delays in their child's development. Parents need to stay objective when it comes to observing their children, especially when it concerns health issues.

One way to detect dyspraxia is by keeping a record of your child's development. Keep a journal or notebook and list down all of your observations. Be diligent in jotting down everything you see for six months. If the symptoms of dyspraxia are present and are consistent throughout this period, then you may have reason to visit your doctor. Your notes will greatly help when you consult with a medical professional.

When the doctor diagnoses for dyspraxia, he will not use any specific tool or test to determine whether your child has the condition. However, he will test for other neurological disorders such as Parkinson's disease, cerebral palsy, multiple sclerosis, and muscular dystrophy. If he tests negative for these neurological conditions, then the doctor will consider dyspraxia as the cause of your child's symptoms. At this point, it is important for every parent to be cooperative and to have an open mind. This time will also be very emotionally challenging for any parent, so it will help to gather emotional support from family and friends.

Here are four important findings that your doctor will consider when diagnosing dyspraxia:

- Delayed motor skills
- Limitations affecting learning and daily life
- Other neurological disorders have been eliminated
- Consistent symptoms from infancy to present age

Once dyspraxia has been confirmed, your doctor will refer your child to other medical professionals who will help him manage the child's symptoms. Your doctor will explain dyspraxia in detail, including how the condition will affect your child's development. He will also enlighten you about the difference that treatment can make on your child's capabilities. If you have questions, never hesitate to ask your doctor. The doctor is the best source of the information you need to confidently undergo this important journey with your child.

Your doctor will explain how a speech therapist can help your child pronounce words more clearly and how a physical therapist and an occupational therapist can help your child accomplish physical tasks that he normally has trouble with. He might also need the help of a psychologist to help him handle the stress and frustrations brought on by the condition.

Expect a series of interviews because medical professionals want to get information directly from you instead of just reading what's in your child's file. Again, it is advised that parents remain cooperative throughout the whole process. Unfortunately, there are other medical conditions related to the occurrence of dyspraxia. Your doctor will also talk to you about other learning difficulties and behavioral problems that your child may exhibit.

Here are other medical conditions that you need to know about:

Dysgraphia

Children with this disorder are unable to write legibly and coherently.

Dyscalculia

This math disorder is characterized by difficulties with numbers and patterns such as the inability to calculate, estimate, and do basic math.

Dyslexia

With this reading disorder, your child may be unable to read words correctly. Writing and spelling can also be affected.

Attention Deficit Hyperactivity Disorder (ADHD)

Children with ADHD will have difficulty concentrating on tasks, staying in one position or place for a long time, and controlling impulses. He also requires constant attention from those around him.

To have your child diagnosed with dyspraxia is not the end of the world. In fact, it is the start of a new chapter in your lives. You and your child will start a journey together and he will need you to be by his side every step of the way. It will help to remember that towards the end of this journey, your goal is to see you child finally living a life of his own—as an independent and self-reliant adult. Your role as parent is to help him achieve that kind of life.

Chapter 4: How a Parent Can Help from Home

The parents of the child with dyspraxia hold the key to a shot at a life that is close-to-normal. Without the necessary support from the child's parents and medical professionals, a child with dyspraxia may be unable to perform simple daily tasks and may continue to need assistance all his life. Consequently, when parents provide all the support and treatment that the child with dyspraxia needs, he will be able to manage his symptoms and will be able to live independently.

In addition to giving your child access to all the treatment he needs, you can still do more for your child in your own home. Here are some tips for parents who have children diagnosed with dyspraxia:

Step 1: Arm Yourself with Knowledge

Read all that you can about the disorder. Absorb every bit of information that the doctors and the therapists tell you. Share this information with your other children, relatives, friends, neighbors, and your child's teachers. The more people around your child know about your youngster's struggles, the better they can adjust to him. With an understanding of dyspraxia, those around your kid will be able to exercise more patience when dealing with him, and in addition they will be able to offer their support.

Step 2: Allow Your Child to Socialize

It's true that it can be hard for your child to meet new friends or to interact with other kids. However, it is still better to let him mingle with other kids and adults rather than to keep him cooped inside the house. Some parents may think that they are protecting their child by homeschooling or not allowing him outside to play with other kids but that could further limit the development of his social skills. Allow your child opportunities to socialize as much as possible. Supervise him if you need to, but don't keep him from hanging out with others.

Step 3: Encourage Sports

Physical activity can be very beneficial for children with dyspraxia. Even if they are prone to stumbling and bumping into things, physical movement will help them develop their motor planning and coordination. Let your child join sports, enjoy games with classmates and friends, or even take up swimming. These activities will also provide opportunities to socialize and meet new friends.

Step 4: Get Your Child a Laptop

Writing with a pen might be difficult for a child with dyspraxia. But that doesn't mean that he cannot put his thoughts down on paper anymore. A computer will allow your child to write down his ideas, and features such as word prediction can help him write faster. It can also fix spelling and grammar automatically so that his writing becomes coherent. However, continue to encourage him to hold a pen and practice his handwriting.

Step 5: Play Games with Your Child

Spend time with your child as much as you can. Play puzzles, building blocks, board games to help develop motor skills. You can also toss a stuffed toy and play catch to help your child improve hand-eye coordination. The key is to manage your expectations as a parent and avoid showing frustration yourself if the child is having difficulty.

Step 6: Teach Your Child to Bake

Children with dyspraxia may not be able to grip objects but parents can help their child develop their hand muscles by allowing them to squeeze things in their hands. Squeezing dough for a pie or pizza can be lots of fun for a child. In addition, they can master the steps of baking if they do it numerous times. Children with dyspraxia have trouble with activities that require a step-by-step process. It helps to talk your child through the steps to help him accomplish tasks such as baking, dressing, brushing his teeth, etc.

Step 7: Make Learning Fun

Learning difficulties are among the symptoms of dyspraxia. Your child may become frustrated when he is unable to write, read, spell, or talk correctly. Provide your kid with pencil grips to help him hold the pen better. Give him colorful pens, markers, scented paper, new books, etc. so that he will not feel discouraged about school and studying. Try to make fun and games a learning opportunity by incorporating lessons in games—balls and blocks can be used to illustrate science concepts like force and motion and cutting up fruit can be used to learn fractions, for example.

Step 8: Help Your Child Build a Healthy Self-Esteem

All children need help from their parents in building a healthy self-esteem. A child with dyspraxia will, perhaps, require more love and attention from his parents and family. Due to the limitations brought on by dyspraxia, a child afflicted with it may feel frustrated, sad, and lose hope. Parents, siblings, teachers should always be there to uplift the child. Encourage your kid to try again but never pressure him to achieve what he is incapable of. Set realistic expectations for your kid and be generous with your praises when he is able to achieve and accomplish tasks. Celebrate every little progress and use setbacks as a prompt for you as parents to try a different method. Provide the proper motivation for your youngster to keep him inspired.

Step 9: Recognize Your Child's Strengths

Your child has strengths that should not be forgotten because of his weaknesses. Although you are working to help him overcome his weaknesses, you should not forget to give him opportunities to show and develop his strengths, too.

Step 10: Talk to Your Child

Your child may be emotionally suffering. Take time to regularly talk to your child about his feelings and emotions. Listen to him and allow him to express how he feels about his condition. He might wonder why he has trouble making friends. Explain to him about his condition and its effects on his body. Be there for your child as a parent and as a friend.

Providing a supportive and loving environment may be one of the best kinds of help that a parent can give to any child. Children with dyspraxia need to feel supported and they need to feel that they will be able to overcome their weaknesses. Parents need to help their child become self-assured and not dependent on other people for the rest of his life.

Chapter 5: A Parent's Journey ~ Coping Advice for Parents

To hear your child diagnosed with any illness is heartbreaking. Since the exact cause of dyspraxia is not known, it hurts moms and dads to think that their child has this disorder for reasons they can never determine. It's tempting to speculate and engage in a blame-game. It is easy to fall into depression, but parents know that their child needs both their presence and support now, more than ever.

Here's some advice for parents of children with dyspraxia. These tips can give you a better outlook and make the journey a lot easier.

Step 1: Get Help

Moms and dads of children with dyspraxia need to support each other. To raise a child with this medical condition can be difficult as it requires a lot of patience and energy. It is physically, emotionally, mentally demanding. Moreover, the treatments that the child will need can be very costly so both parents need to find resources in order to support the medical needs of the child. In case of single parents, assemble a support group of relatives and friends from whom to request assistance. There are also organizations that provide financial support for single parents and children with illnesses.

Step 2: Join a Support Network

Get in touch with other parents. Search for a dyspraxia group in your area and join. Parents of kids with dyspraxia can share experiences and information, swap advice, and offer financial help. They ould also offer moral support and help you stay focused on your child's improvement.

Step 3: Talk to Someone

During your journey, you might find it difficult to stay positive and to keep an optimistic attitude towards life. The stress from caring for your child on a daily basis can take its toll on you and you may end up a wreck. Make sure that you don't neglect your physical, emotional, and mental health. Talk to someone you trust or consult with a therapist to help you get through your own struggles.

Step 4: Take Care of Yourself

Because your child needs you, you cannot fall ill. Eat right, exercise, and get enough sleep. Find time to rest and relax even when you have to care for your child full-time. If possible, get some time off at least once a week. A caring family member could watch over your child for a few hours while you get some needed me-time. When you are healthy and you have a good disposition, you can look out for your child better.

Step 5: Work towards Acceptance and Peace

It's natural to get angry and start waging wars on everything for your child's condition. However, no one is to blame. Not you, not your husband, not God, and not your neighbors. The best way to have a happier life for you and your child is to accept your circumstance. Stop being angry at your situation and work to attain inner peace. Once you are at peace, you can look at events in your life positively and this attitude will also have a big effect on your child and family.

Caring for a sick child can be challenging. Parents will tend to forget their own health and needs when their youngsters are ill. However, parents of children with dyspraxia need to remember that their children will need them, possibly for a long time, and so they need to be there for their kid. Therefore, they must always strive to have a healthy and strong body and mind in order to adequately provide the needs of their child.

Conclusion

Dyspraxia is not like a cold that will go away after some time. Children diagnosed with dyspraxia will still have it until adulthood. They will have to be able to manage the symptoms so that they are able to live as independent individuals. All parents have the duty to teach their young children life skills so that they can fend for themselves when they grow up. In the case of the parents of children with dyspraxia, they will need to provide their child with physical therapy, speech therapy, and occupational therapy, too.

Parents of children with dyspraxia should never lose hope, though. The journey will be long and challenging, but in time, it will be a fruitful one. With a loving environment, parent support, and professional treatment, the child with dyspraxia can live independently and he will be able to make a life for himself without constant assistance from others.

In this journey, the best support that a parent can ever provide for his child is his unwavering presence. Parents need to be there for their children physically, emotionally, and mentally. It's not enough to pay for the treatments and to pay people to assist him throughout his life. A child with dyspraxia will need attention, love, and care from his parents more than anything.

Finally, I'd like to thank you for purchasing this book! If you found it helpful, I'd greatly appreciate it if you'd take a moment to leave a review on Amazon. Thank you!

Made in the USA
Lexington, KY
31 July 2017